CHAPTER 1

Money

Money is simply a bartering medium. You do something useful for someone (e.g., work) and they give you money in return. You then take your money to a store to buy things that you need (e.g., spend money on groceries). You need the groceries and the only acceptable bartering medium at the grocery store is money, therefore; you get a job and work to earn money. If the grocery store accepted, let's say, rocks for groceries, then you could go collect rocks and use them to buy/barter for the groceries. It would still take you time and effort to collect rocks, so we can still consider that "working". We need to understand what money represents and how money works to be able to further understand personal finance. If you do not understand money, you will have a very difficult time understanding how credit cards work or how the stock market works.

I am not writing this book to claim that money is the source of all of happiness. I am not here to tell you that you need to work, work, work and not enjoy life. I am here to inform you, in simple terms, how money works, how to use money to your advantage, how to let money work for you, and how to properly understand and control your personal finance. Whatever your goals are in life, you will achieve them faster and with greater percent chance of success if you can keep your finances in order and understand the value of money.

We have heard people tell us to "value a dollar" or tell us that "time is money." We need to understand more deeply rather than just repeat these simple 3-word sayings. Value a dollar. This is good to keep in the back of our minds, but what does this mean?

Technically the value of the dollar is ever-changing due to inflation and exchange rates and price fluctuations, but this saying
helps us in the broad sense of value our earnings so we can barter
for things that we need and want. One dollar used to be worth
more than it is today due to inflation. You could buy a loaf of bread
for a nickel or a gallon of milk for a quarter. Today you might pay
three dollars for a loaf of bread and five dollars for a gallon a milk.
We have to remember that back in the day people's wages were
much lower. Let's say people were making ten dollars a day working at the steel mill and now, those same people could be making
two hundred dollars a day. Regardless of the exact math, I'm just
trying to help you wrap your head around inflation. For those
of you with a business background, some of these early teaching
points may seem obvious, but not all of us had the opportunity
to learn business terms. Bear with these initial observations, I`m
trying to level the playing field so that anyone can understand my
ideas and in turn understand personal finance.

For later topics throughout this book, we will be assuming
inflation always exists and needs to be taken into account when
deciding things like how much money do you need to retire or
what the value of a dollar might be in the future. As long as you
understand that year over year, one dollar continuously declines
in absolute value because inflation exists and the price of goods
will slowly rise over time, you are good to go.

Let`s get back to valuing a dollar. We need to value money
because it is more or less the only acceptable form of bartering. (I
realize you can still barter items for items in some places and there
can be a few exceptions to this broad assumption, but I am using
the United States as my general area of information and more
often than not, you need money to acquire other things. Even if
you are handy and can build a table or knit a sweater, you still need
money to buy the supplies to make those items.) If we can teach
our brain to value money appropriately, then we have the begin-
nings of a successful and prosperous understanding of personal
finance.

Circling back to our other simple saying, time is money, we

know it takes time to work and we need to work to earn money, therefore we need time to earn money. Sounds easy enough, but we need to put that into practice when spending money and not just when earning money. This will help us comprehend the cost of spending money. Everyone earns different amounts and spends different amounts, but we all have a cost associated with spending money, and that's time. People wish for more hours in a day or more years on their life, the former is mathematically impossible, and the latter has infinite variables, but you can control time in terms of spending. We can all make choices that could help us live longer, but until we value money and understand that time costs money, we cannot "buy" ourselves a longer life.

Let's say you want to exercise more to become healthier and in turn live longer. Exercising takes time; time is money; so, exercising costs money. This might start to sound a little abstract, but I want to illustrate that all decisions have costs. If you own a business that sells pizza and you decide to close at 8pm instead of at 9pm because you want to go exercise for an hour, you`ve now lost 1 hour of potential revenue. Let's say that exercise for this pizza shop owner costs him or her 1 hours' worth of revenue (aka money). In later chapters, we will see how we can use time to let money work for us. It's kind of a funny thing; the more money you earn, the more money time starts to cost. If the pizza shop would earn $100 in that hour the owner decides to close, then exercising costs him or her $100. If the shop would earn $500 in that hour, now exercising has become more expensive and costs him or her $500.

I am not trying to convince you that you need to be rich, but that you need to understand how money works in order to make financial decisions correctly and in the best interest of you and your family. When someone says they want to be rich, most likely what they want is financial freedom. The freedom to do or buy what you want without worrying about the cost. If you do not necessarily want a fancy sports car or an oversized mansion on the coastline, then financial freedom will be much easier and faster to obtain. The more things you want, the more money you need. The more money you need, the more money you must earn. The more money you earn, the more time costs. Think about that.

CHAPTER 2

Save

Saving is a huge part of building wealth and gaining financial freedom. It is much, much easier to spend than to save which makes this part of building wealth very difficult for countless people. I like to use the saying, "It is not about how much money you make; it is about how much money you have." What I am trying to illustrate with this quote is that rich people can be bad at saving too, people compare salaries too much and use them as an excuse as to why they cannot save, and in the end, what matters when trying to gain financial freedom is how much money you have, not how many cool things you own or how many luxurious vacations you have taken.

The first big step to reaching any sense of financial freedom is having an emergency fund. You need to figure out your monthly expenses first. On average, in one month, how much money do you spend. Include everything; rent, car payment, TV, phone, utilities, food (groceries and restaurants), shopping, etc., etc. An emergency fund of at least 3 months' worth of spending will put you in a great starting place. Mentally you will begin to be at ease. This emergency fund is there in case of a possible medical emergency or maybe you get laid off from work unexpectedly or maybe a large appliance breaks at your house, or maybe, just maybe there's even a global pandemic. If you use any part of your emergency fund, you should refill it as quick as possible. Three months' worth of funds is a great start, if you can get to six months, you will be in amazing shape financially and mentally. From there, you can start to invest your extra savings and fast track yourself to financial freedom. You cannot start to invest until you have built an emergency fund. The emergency money needs to be liquid (aka accessible at any time) in case of an emergency, hence the name.

Financial freedom is when you have enough money to live off of your investments and/or your passive income. You can reach financial freedom by investing so much in the stock market, for example, that you are nearly certain you could live year to year off of the returns you make, or you could own one or more businesses in which they operate automatically and produce enough profit for you to live without any other money. Remember that financial freedom must cover your yearly expenses, so if your expenses are high, you will need more money to reach the same goal as someone who has fewer expenses. Financial freedom allows you to do what you want to do, when you want to do it. You want to go see your family across the country? No problem, your investments or businesses are working for you no matter where you are or what you are doing. This is the goal; you do not have to rely on working in a specific place at a specific time to live the way you want to live and spend the way you want to spend. If you spend a lot, you will need more money to reach financial freedom, but that is fine. We all have different ways of living and being happy. In this case, you may just need to work harder or take more risks or work more hours/years to get to your financial freedom, and that is a cost you are willing to have to spend in order to live the way you want.

Let's revert back to that saying, "it is not about how much money you make; it is about how much money you have". We can use some numeric values to show what I mean. Billy makes $80,000 a year (don't worry about taxes or other considerations, I just want to use simple examples to make my point). Billy likes to go out to eat and likes to buy the newest tech gadgets and drink high-end alcohol. Billy buys his friends rounds of drinks when they go out and always takes the private Uber ride instead of the pool option. He lives by himself in a really nice apartment and leases a luxurious Mercedes. At the end of the year, Billy was only able to save $2,000 after all of his other expenses piled up. Jim on the other hand doesn't have as high a paying job, he makes $60,000 a year. Jim has a couple of roommates which helps keep his rent cost down. He doesn't even own a car; he can bike or take the metro to his job. Jim takes a little extra time to go to the grocery store and cooks almost all his meals. He'll go out to the bar, but he'll make sure to have a couple drinks at home first so maybe he just buys 1 or 2 drinks for himself while he is out dancing and having a good time. Jim has an older phone, but it works for what he needs, his job gave him a laptop if he needs to use it and other than that, doesn't get too excited by new technology. At the end of the year, Jim was able to save $15,000. Jim and Billy are actually really good friends. They watch the football games together, they go to the gym, and they go out for drinks with the same group of people. Billy "lives it up", he buys nicer things, he likes to be served at the restaurant, and he doesn't hesitate to buy the newest phone. At the end of the day, Jim and Billy have the same friends, live in the same area, and both enjoy life. The difference is that Jim saved $13,000 more than Billy this year even though Billy earned $20,000 more.

And just for the sake of seeing the numbers, let's assume these two had the same jobs and spending habits for 10 years. Now Billy has saved only $20,000 and Jim has saved an impressive $130,000. Jim makes less money, but is much closer to financial freedom than Billy. To show you even greater disparity let me add in some compounding interest. Let us assume that these two guys put their savings every month into the stock market and earn 8% a year in growth. After that 10-year period, Billy would have about $33,000 saved and Jim would have an astounding $221,000 saved.

Billy makes more money than Jim, how could this even be possible? Save and invest. That's how. I find that most people will not argue with you if you tell them that they probably need to save more money and that they need to invest. I remind them; don't you want to retire and reach financial freedom someday? Plenty of people make enough money to start saving and investing. The problem is when it comes to putting the act of saving into practice. Like I said earlier, it is much much easier to spend than to save.

It might take you 3 months to save $1,000, but it could easily take you less than 3 minutes to spend it. You get your paycheck (cha ching!) you send a group text to your friends saying you just bought a new TV, and they should all come over this weekend. What was wrong with your old TV? You just bought it last year. The temptations to buy are hard to avoid. Many people have jobs where their goal is to get you to buy something from them. If we start to think about this before buying something, it may help us avoid spending unnecessary money. Whether you are at the store or browsing food options for delivery or watching TV and see an ad come on the screen, you are being targeted to spend money.

Marketing teams get paid a lot of money to make their product look amazing or seem necessary to have and they use sales techniques to make you believe you are getting a deal you just cannot pass up. Let us look at food delivery. You open an app and right away you see a "deal", something like "order today and get 75% off your delivery fee!" Sounds amazing, 75% off of anything sounds like an incredible deal. What you maybe do not realize is that the delivery fee is only $4. Yes, you will save $3 off that delivery fee, but don't forget you still need to pay the service fee, processing fee and maybe even tip the driver. You were thinking about cooking your dinner which might have cost $4-$5 dollars, but because you just wanted to see what good deals you could find on delivery, you're suddenly spending $20 for a meal you did not even want that badly. That "deal" actually ended up costing you an extra $15 compared to cooking the meal yourself.

You were hungry and needed food, we can't get past that, but your act of skimming for a deal actually set you back $15 for the same result; your hunger is gone. This is an everyday example and only a small savings but imagine you did this 3 times a week. Now you're talking about $45 a week or even worse, $2,340 a year. Move the comma one spot to see the cost over 10 years: $23,400 you spent, just because you thought you were "saving" 75%. Crazy to think about.

We could use similar examples in everyday life to show the same result. Instead of self-parking, you decide to valet; a $15 difference. See the same numbers used above. You got a private Uber ride instead of the Pool option; a $15 difference. Now you can start to see how all of these seemingly harmless decisions during a regular week can really add up. I don't need to list hundreds of examples of where you might be over-spending, there are plenty of blogs that can give you advice and tips on that. What I want to try and help you do is see the big picture and really understand how money and savings work and change your mindset from not caring or knowing about these decisions, to thoughtfully putting them into practice and really demanding your brain to see how numbers compound when making a series of small decisions.

Those numbers of money spent on food delivery would look even crazier if instead of spending the extra $15 on the delivered meal, you actually took that $15 and invested it. It's good to have not spent it, now you have $15 more than you would have, but investing it is the next step. Quickly, let me show the numeric difference. We would have saved $23,400 over 10 years by making a good decision about a $15 swing 3 times a week. Now if we turned around and invested that money at the 8% rate of return, we've been using, that now turns into $31,300. It is easy to understand that if these small decisions on savings can have such a significant impact, then even bigger savings will have a bigger impact.

Instead of buying that new TV with your paycheck, what if you invested that money instead? Instead of buying those new shoes that you probably won't ever wear because they are kind of uncomfortable, you invested that money instead. If you can start to see all your purchases as possible missed investment opportunities, you will start to naturally save more and invest more and grow your personal wealth.

One quick shortcut I like to use myself when making purchasing decisions, is to decide how many more days of work I will have to endure before I can retire because of buying a certain item. We are going to assume that your invested money doubles every 10 years (it could double faster or slower depending on your risk tolerance and market returns, blah blah blah). Stay with me here. What I'm assuming is that any savings decision you make right now, (assuming you then invest the money instead), will double in value every 10 years.

Let's look at another example. I'm thinking about buying the new version of a video game that just came out. It's $60 and looks cool, but it is essentially the same as the one I have. If I use my shortcut, I start to calculate that if I spend $60 today to buy this game that I don't really need, it would be like losing $120 10 years from now (doubled in value), or like losing $240 20 years from now (doubled again), or like losing $480 30 years from now. Let us assume I'm around 25 years old and trying to retire around 55 years old. My video game decision will cost my retired self $480. I usually assume I could live off of $150 a day in retirement. Therefore, deciding whether to buy my new video game or not is going to essentially cost me 3 whole days of retirement. This means I would have to work 3 extra days of my life because I want to buy a new game that is essentially the same as the one I already own.

Coming full circle, let us use that TV as an example to amplify the cost of a possible purchase. To make the math easy we can say the TV we were debating about buying with our paycheck was going to cost $600. Double that 3 times and we have $4,800 as the cost of buying the TV in retirement. Divide that by the $150 a day it costs to live in retirement, and we have 32 days of work we will have to add to our lives before retirement just so we can buy the new TV, when we didn't even really need it in the first place. You have to tack on an entire month of extra work because you wanted to upgrade your 1-year-old TV. Do you still think it was a good financial decision to buy it?

In conclusion, saving money is essential to growing wealth and becoming financially free. I've given you some quick math examples to use when deciding about making purchases. Small purchases often can add up to a large one-off purchase, so try to think about your spending options every time you go to pull out your credit card or hit "confirm purchase" on a delivery food app. Saving money is a lifestyle, one time here and one time there is better than not saving at all, but to truly save money as a tool to build wealth, it needs to be a daily routine. Stop being lazy and overpaying for convenience unless it's truly valuable to you. Stop buying things you do not really need or will not really use, and stop giving in to social norms and using them as an excuse to spend money.

Just because someone buys a round of drinks does not mean you have to do the same in return. That was their choice to spend their money, don't let the social norm or social pressure of returning the favor allow your friends to essentially decide how you are going to spend your hard-earned money. Maybe that friend has already reached financial freedom or maybe they have a different way of reaching it (like working more hours or taking more risks). Your friends are your friends whether you buy them a drink or not, trust me, otherwise they are not really your friend at all.

It might not be cool to share an Uber with strangers, but it is pretty cool to retire at the age of 45. Saving money is very much a mental struggle. Try to win the struggle as often as possible, and you will reap the benefits soon enough. And the benefits are greater than any video game or delivered meal. Financial freedom is worth it. Work hard, save hard, invest hard.

CHAPTER 3

Credit Cards

Credit cards represent money and have become an easier way to purchase items. The grocery store accepts credit cards instead of dollars because they trust the credit card companies will pay them for your purchase on your behalf, in dollars. It is a slightly delayed payment to the grocery store vs receiving cold hard cash directly from the customer, but it is reliable and has become the norm.

What you, as a spender, need to understand is that when you swipe your credit card, you are officially borrowing money from the credit card company and you are legally obligated to pay them back. This is why credit card companies give different people a different maximum credit line, or simply, they tell you how much money they will let you borrow at any given time. When you apply for a credit card, the company will run your credit report and essentially decide how much they trust you. The more the perceived trust, the more money they will let you borrow.

Don't forget that credit card companies are "for profit" businesses. They are not government owned and they are not put in place only as a favor to consumers. They want to earn money, just like any other business. The way they do this is by charging you interest on money you don't pay back in the agreed amount of time.

We need to start thinking of credit cards as a helpful tool to build our credit score and as a way to buy expensive things without having to hold large sums of cash in your pockets. They are not free money or tools to buy things you want that you cannot afford. No matter your financial position, it is useful to know how credit cards function. When you apply for and then accept a credit card, you are entering a legal contract. The credit card company lends you money and you agree to pay it back (usually within a month); otherwise, you have agreed to pay interest on the borrowed sum.

Sometimes these interest rates are insane, the current national average is about 20% annually. To illustrate how this works using real world examples vs. theory, let's look at a numeric example. So, you go to the grocery store, you do your shopping, and you get to the checkout line. The clerk scans all your items and tells you that the total is $100. Your choices for payment would be cash; where you take a one hundred dollar bill out of your wallet and hand it to the clerk and that barter trade/purchase is finished. The grocery store set the price of their products, you agreed to the price and paid cash, simple.

Another option would be a debit card. This option is identical to cash, the clerk swipes your debit card and money is withdrawn immediately from your debit account and put into the grocery store bank account. People use debit cards, so they don't have to carry cash and can more securely carry money around. If they lose their debit card, they could cancel the card. If they lose their cash, tough luck.

The third option for payment and the one we are focusing on is when you pull your credit card out of your purse or wallet and pay with that. Like we said before, the grocery store accepts this payment from the credit card company and will receive payment likely at the end of the day. This is all fine and good, the grocery store and the credit card company have a deal in place for processing fees and payment schedules and what not. What we care about is what is happening to you. You swiped the credit card so now you`re on the hook for $100 that will need to be paid back to the credit card company. This payment will eventually come out of your checking/debit account of your bank, same that it would have if you just used your debit card instead of your credit card. However, the benefit you miss out on by using cash or a debit card is building your credit score and building trust with your credit card company.

I want you to change your understanding here at this pivotal point. You have decided to use the credit card and borrow the money for the time being because you want to prove to the credit card company that you are trustworthy in paying back your debts. You need to build a line of credit so that later in life you can borrow larger sums of money. $100 may not seem like a lot to borrow, but you have to start somewhere. You borrow $100 here and $100 there and keep paying on time and next thing you know; the credit card company has emailed you saying they will raise your limit (and that now you can borrow more money at a time). This will help when you start to want to buy more expensive things. Farther down the road, the benefit of using your credit card and paying it on time and using your credit card and paying it on time, is that your credit score continues to improve. Now you want to buy a car or a house and need a bank to lend you money. They will run your credit report to find out your credit score and see that they can trust you to make payments on time. A lender will structure a payment plan for you to borrow let's say $200,000 for a new house at a low interest rate, and all is well in the world. You get your dream home with borrowed money and the bank gets their interest payments on time with no hassle.

Now let's go back a bit. You swiped your credit card at the grocery store for $100 and you're on the hook with the credit card company because you borrowed that $100 from them. You take your groceries home and can enjoy them right away. That's great, you still have the same amount of cash in your wallet and the same amount of money in your checking/debit account as you did before you went to the grocery store. The only difference is now you owe the credit card company $100. Nowadays you can look at your transactions online, all the credit card companies make it pretty user friendly. Your charge at the grocery store will be pending for a couple days and then will be accepted and processed and your total due amount will change from $0 to $100.

You can pay off your credit card immediately if you'd like. For me, this is the best advice. Every few days, as new charges come through, just keep paying them off in full. Wait another few day, pay off in full again. You keep your debt at or near zero at all times and you can rest easy knowing that you do not owe anyone any money. You have your checking account linked up directly to the credit card app and boom, the credit card company gets their $100 that they let you borrow, and you get debited the $100 from your account just like if you had used your debit card, but now you've gotten the added benefit of helping to earn trust from the credit card company and improve your credit score. In this scenario, you end up spending the same amount while getting the added benefit of a better credit score and eventually in the long run an opportunity to borrow a large sum of money for a large purchase.

Let us go back a little bit again. You made the $100 purchase on your credit card at the grocery store. It took a couple days to process and now your credit card company says you owe them $100. You decide not to pay it off immediately and you see on their app they tell you that you must make a minimum payment by the end of the month of $30 to avoid being charged a late fee. Ok, that's fine, we can pay $30 before the end of the month and carry over the remaining $70 to the next statement cycle. If you really can't pay the full amount, then this option is the next best choice. You're basically just extending the borrowing period and the credit card company still trusts that you'll pay the $70 soon enough. Unfortunately, you will have to pay interest on the remaining $70. You avoid the late fee and most likely your credit score will not be affected negatively. The issue is now you owe about $71.12 because of the 20% annual interest rate (I divided 20 by 12 to get the monthly rate. Some credit companies will even get as particular as charging you the average daily interest, but there is no need to complicate the math for our purpose here) and you're out of food and have to go back to the grocery store again.

You spend another $100 on food and now you owe $171.12. $71.12 from last month and $100 from this month. We haven't had to pay a late fee or hurt our credit score yet, but you can see how this can be a bad habit where you get yourself into a hole of owing an increasing amount of money when all you did was buy groceries. You can now see that you owe $171.12. You make the minimum payment of $30 again at the end of the month and you only owe $141.12. Here comes the interest again, since you have a balance, the credit card company is going to charge you interest. Now your total amount owed is $143.38.

Just so we remember, we swiped twice for $100 each, so we spent $200. We paid the $30 minimum twice (aka $60), so without interest we should only owe $140. It's a $3.38 loss for not paying off our balance. Now you're hungry again and need food so back to the grocery store you go, and you swipe your credit card for $100. Now you owe $243.38. This is where people start to feel trapped. Today you swiped for $100, but somehow, you owe $243.38. That doesn't seem fair. Well, you never paid off your first two borrowings of $100 each and the credit card company doesn't just forget about that as time goes on. (I want to make a quick interjection here and say that some credit card companies do have a 0% annual interest rate for let's say the first year of the using the card. This is a nice deal, but make sure to set a reminder on when the 0% all of a sudden will jump to 20% and make sure to pay off your balance)

I am using a simple example here with the groceries, but imagine it's your groceries and your car insurance, and the few times you went out to a restaurant, and went to the movies, and bought new clothes, etc., etc. Move the decimal point over two spots on each of all those numbers and you can really start to understand how a lot of people get caught up in credit card debt. You're swiping and swiping and making minimum payments and swiping and swiping. The next thing you know the credit card app tells you that you owe $24,338 and you feel like you can never ever pay it off.

Let me repeat myself again when I make these crucial points, we need to change our mindset with respect to credit cards. They are tools to build credit, not tools to buy things that we cannot afford. To recap, ideally you swipe your card for a purchase and as soon as payments are processed (no longer pending) you pay off the card direct from your checking/debit account. When this is not possible, we have agreed to make the monthly minimum payment to avoid paying late fees and damaging our credit score. Hopefully you just do this one time and then you get back on track and pay the balance back to zero again. Remember, the borrowed amount will continue to accumulate and will need to be paid off at some point.

Now let's get into the third scenario, the one you want to avoid completely and at all costs. You swipe your credit card at the grocery store for $100. You get to take the food home and enjoy it right away without being debited the $100 from your account. Now, here comes the end of the month and the credit card company wants their $100 back. Let's talk about two possibilities that have the same outcome. One, you simply forget to check how much you owe and never send the payment to the credit card company. Two, you know that you owe the money, but actually do not have the funds in your checking account to pay for the borrowed amount.

Scenario one is easy to fix, set a reminder in your phone to check your credit card balance every month before the payment is due and make sure you pay it off. Or, if you are confident that you always have the money in your checking account ready to pay the credit card, you can set up auto-pay. Scenario two is not so easy to fix. In the previous chapter I have covered ways to save money and later in the book I will cover alternate ways to earn more money, both of which could help with scenario two.

Now let me explain with numbers the cost of not making any payment at all on your credit card bill. You owe $100, but do not pay anything. Interest rate is 20% annually and late fee is $20. Now you owe $121.60. Second month you swipe $100 at the grocery store. New balance is $221.60. You do not make any payment again. Now you owe $221.60 + $3.55 (interest) + $20 (late fee again) = $245.15. Another month, another $100 at the grocery store, now we are at $345.15. Again, we do not pay anything off the bill, and we have $345.15 + $5.52 (interest) + $20 (late fee) = $370.67. We spent $300 at the grocery store and now we owe $370.67. See how improper use of your credit card can be very costly? That is the dollar penalty of misusing the card, you pay more than what the items really cost. Secondly, is the damage to your credit score. Depending what your score was in the first place, in this scenario your score could easily drop 25-100 points. Long story short, do not abuse your credit cards. Use them as tools to improve your credit score. If you do not have the funds to pay for something, do not use your credit card as "free money". It will come back to haunt you.

CHAPTER 4

Stocks

We are always hearing people complain that the rich keep getting richer. Stocks and investing are a big part of what contributes to that. Nowadays, the market has become more accessible than ever before. Access is good, but knowledge is important to get the most out of that access. The playing field has mostly leveled for everyday investors, and now individual investing is just a matter of understanding how the stock market actually works.

In my opinion, this is something that should be taught early and often in the education system. When you purchase a stock of a company, e.g. Disney, you're really buying a share of ownership. Way back when (1957), Disney decided to issue shares through an IPO. For the sake of this chapter, we do not really need to fully understand all the technical terms, but what we need to understand is what we bought and how we use it to earn money/build wealth.

Ok, so, we buy a share of Disney from another investor who was looking to sell their share. Now we own a share of the company and as investors see that the company is doing well and turning big profits and announcing new products, the company and its shares becomes more valuable. We can wait a while and if we think the company has reached its peak of value, we could sell our share to another investor and take our profits.

I personally never buy shares of individual companies because it is known to be riskier. Disney is a powerhouse company, more than likely if you buy Disney, you will make a profit in the long run; however, when you start to look at smaller companies that have higher potential for growth, the likelihood of success starts to decline. This is common sense. The riskier you are, the higher possible return you could receive, but there is a higher probability of losing as well.

Diversification is essential to building sustainable wealth. It is widely accepted that diversification is a good thing. You want to own some risky stocks, some big company stocks, some foreign stocks, some in the tech sector, some in the real estate sector, etc. etc. I am not a professional money advisor, so I do not want to give you direct advice on what exact companies to buy or when to buy them. The point I want to get across is how the stock market works and the general rules to follow. My goal is to get you interested enough and knowledgeable enough to go out there and open an account and start to invest.

There is plenty of research to be done and information to sift through, but first, you need to understand the basics and really engage yourself by opening an account. Let's reiterate again, diversification is a major key to sustainability. Exactly how much of this and how much of that to buy is better left up to the professionals, but I want to make sure you are becoming interested enough to do further research and follow up by buying into the market.

You will have many other choices than just single company stocks like Disney. Personally, I buy groups of many stocks that are packed into a portfolio called a mutual fund and more recently we have been given the options of ETFs. What happens here is that I buy a share of a fund that has holdings in let's say 500 different companies. I like this buying strategy because the mutual fund does the diversification for you. I buy one share, but it is like buying tiny shares of 500 different companies. So, if one company is performing badly, I still have 499 other companies that can make up for that one.

A difficult part for a lot of people is that when you buy mutual funds, the strategy is more along the lines of buy and hold and the time horizon to see success is long. In today's world, people have become more impatient. They want instant results and that is a risky play when it comes to the stock market. On any given day a single stock could drop 10, 20, 30 percent and bye-bye goes your money. On the contrary, over time, the broad market brings positive returns historically. The S&P 500 has never been unable to get back to its all-time high. Meaning, over the past 100 years, the broad market has eventually turned a profit for any investor that bought and held low-risk, ultra-diversified funds.

I want to clarify that I am talking about mutual funds that are made up of hundreds of companies. The S&P 500 being the most well-known. Certainly, there are single stocks that have failed and declined and never became worth what they once were, but when we are talking about the broad diversified funds like a S&P 500 mutual fund (which is comprised of the largest 500 companies in the US), we have always seen a positive return over long stretches of time. The buy and hold strategy will not get you rich overnight, but it allows certainty of positive gains and allows you to carry-on with your everyday life without worrying about having to sell your stocks at a certain time.

It has never been my day job to study stocks or trade stocks. So, why would I think that I could outsmart the broad market and randomly buy into a company and then turn around and know when to sell? Being risk-averse might sound boring, but it is a proven strategy that just takes time and patience. We were using an example earlier in this book in which we said that your money, when put into the broad market, will double every 10 years. That happens without you having to do any research, take any big risks, or check on your funds day in and day out. All we have to do is open an account, start saving and let our money do the work. It really is simple.

If you are reading this book and do not even have a brokerage account or IRA set-up, here is my best advice; ask your friends who do or do a little research and find a company that you would like to open an account with. I personally use Vanguard because of its low fees and user-friendly set-up, but Vanguard does have some higher minimums for mutual funds that maybe some new apps like Robinhood might not. Regardless of what company you choose, open an account and just buy some shares of an S&P 500 mutual fund or ETF they offer on your particular interface. This is the start to you building wealth.

What is great about this way of building wealth is that you do not need to be a genius, you do not need to invent something, you do not need to be an athlete or famous actor, you just need to be disciplined with your money and come up with a systematic way to invest your money. Then you sit back, relax, and reap the benefits over time. You will see that with just your first purchase of a mutual fund, you will become more interested in how it all works. You will do more research; you will see your fund grow little by little and want to put more money in and watch it grow more and more. You will start to hit milestones, like when your account value hits $1,000, then again at $2,000 and again at $5,000 and $10,000 and so on and so on until you hit a number that gets you to financial freedom.

Do not be discouraged by lack of knowledge or by lack of funds to invest. It is very easy and there are many ways to start with small investments. It is never too late to start investing this way, but the earlier you start the better. You now have the knowledge of compound interest and we have discussed that your money should double every 10 years, so every year earlier that you start is another year you get to earn interest and get to start the doubling process. Me, I bought my first investment at age 20. One of my college professors told me that if there was anything I should take away from his class, it's that I should go home and open a Vanguard brokerage account and start investing. I did. And wow, am I glad I did. I still to this day have not sold my initial purchase, 10 years later and what would you know, that initial purchase has more than doubled in value.

I was always interested in money growing up, I would ask questions to my dad and my uncle and my friend's parents about what the stock market was and how it worked. The best advice I ever received was exactly what I just told to you, open a brokerage account and start investing. There are all kinds of fancy words and fancy jobs that deal with the stock market. It all can seem very intimidating, but the bare bones of how it works is very simple. You invest your money in shares of different companies, those companies grow and as they succeed, your shares of those companies become worth more money.

Build your emergency fund equal to six months of living expenses and then every month, whatever amount of money you have over top of that emergency fund, invest into the market. You can come up with a system that fits you, but an easy example would be if we say your monthly living expense is $3,000, we multiply by 6 and say that your emergency fund should be $18,000 in a liquid form (aka cash, savings account, or checking account). Then once we have built our checking account balance to $18,000, we wait for the 1st day of each month and any amount of money we have north of $18,000 we take it and invest it. Some months it might be $300, some months it might be $800, and just remember that if your emergency fund drops below $18,000, wait for it to refill before investing. Work hard, save hard, invest hard.

CHAPTER 5

Side Hustle

There are all different ways to earn money. There are all different types of people with all different kinds of skills. Regardless of your full-time job, having a side hustle is a great way to earn more money, possibly give yourself a creative outlet, keep busy, try something new, or get back into something you used to enjoy.

Many popular side hustle gigs of the past few years have been peer to peer business opportunities like driving for Uber, renting your spare bedroom on Airbnb, or letting a stranger take your convertible for a ride on a car rental app like Turo. These are great side hustle choices when you already have acquired the large purchase item like a house or car and earn money renting or driving while still being able to use that item yourself as you need it. However, if you do not already own that large purchase item, it can be expensive to break into these kinds of side hustles.

Food delivery is a great option for some people because you might just need a scooter or bicycle and can do it on your own time. Having a side hustle gives you that little extra boost in income that can help you see savings/investing results at a faster rate. I could list plenty of side hustle ideas, but really, I just want to get you into the mindset of having that hustle attitude towards earning, saving, and investing. Even those of us that have a 9-5 job still have an opportunity to create a side hustle. How many hours a week do you find yourself watching TV or scrolling social media or just flat out bored? Having a side hustle keeps your brain functioning at a higher level and gives us a little extra money to invest.

We have established that we want to save as much as we can while still enjoying life and that we want to invest early and often in life to reap the benefits of compounding interest, so the side hustle is that much more important when you are young, have the energy, and have the time to do it. My main side hustle over the past 15 years has been video filming and editing. I would take gigs back in the day that might take me 5 or more hours to complete and were only paying $50. But it was the hustle that kept me going, I would learn more and meet more people and get better and better and soon enough I could charge people $500 for a project that would take me 5 hours to complete. It was a great choice of a side hustle for me because I enjoyed the craft, had some education in it, and could complete a lot of the projects on my own time. I could use the artsy, creative side of my brain while my day-to-day job was more repetitive and constant.

As my regular job was becoming more time consuming, I would hire people to do the filming for me and I would just take on the editing, because I no longer had the flexibility to be at the filming location and be at my regular job. Still, I found a way to keep the hustle alive. For a brief time, I did rent my Jeep Wrangler on Turo (the Airbnb of car rentals). It was not my intent when purchasing the vehicle but proved to be another source of income before deciding to sell the vehicle all together.

If we apply some numeric examples, we can see how a little side income can really add up. Let's say you could make $200 a week with our side hustle. Some weeks you have a lot of extra time and can make more while other weeks you have plans with friends or maybe are on vacation or just do not have the projects lined up. Just a mere $200 a week invested over 10 years would give us about $35,000 in extra savings. If you had the stamina to pull it off for 20 years, then you're looking at $110,000. And all this extra money is in addition to your regular salary and investment. You can easily see how much faster you could get to financial freedom by having a side hustle. Plus, besides the financial gains, you have secondary gains such as creativity, improving business sense, even exercise if you're delivering food on a bike or maybe doing yoga classes on YouTube.

I cannot tell you what side hustle is best for you, but I

can encourage you to find one. If you are someone that regularly spends most of your normal paycheck, having a side hustle can act as a savings tool. You can separate your side hustle earnings from your regular paycheck amount and say to yourself that everything you earn doing your side gig will go directly into investments. This is where you have to be disciplined. This is a key step. You have to avoid the trap; just because you make more money does not mean you should go out and spend more money. You have decided to use some of your free time to make money with your side hustle and you should care enough about your future to put that money to work.

I want to emphasize again that saving early in life helps a lot later in life. It may not seem that bad to live without savings when you are 20 or 30 years old, but these are the key years to start amassing your nest egg and enjoying the benefits of compounding interest. Plus, you are probably not worried about children or buying property and hopefully your day job has not caused too much stress yet. You have the energy and time to spend on a side hustle.

Don't wait to start saving. I am not saying you should choose your side hustle over spending time with family and friends, but if you manage your time responsibly, you can do both and rake in some extra investment funds. Be careful with the YOLO (you only live once) and "treat yourself" attitudes that get thrown around social media all the time. You can have a good time and see the world and experience new things and meet new people and still save money. Trust me, I did it. The side hustle is a good tool to keep yourself busy and keep yourself earning money. It is all part of the greater goal, financial freedom. Side hustle and save.

CHAPTER 6

Taxes

The word "tax" has quite the negative connotation to it. You get your first paycheck and thought you were making $4,000 a month and bam, the check gets deposited into your account and its only $3,200. You think to yourself, what happened to 20% of my money? I did all the work and did not get paid what I was promised. Well, taxes are something we should understand so we can prepare for the after-tax payment from our employer and not be so surprised when we make $800 less than we expected. Also, taxes can be even more tricky when talking about our side hustle.

Let's start with our paycheck. You are most likely a W-2 employee. Otherwise, you could be a 1099 independent contractor, in which your tax situation would be a bit different. W-2 employees have federal income tax (in some states, state income tax too) and payroll tax deductions taken out of their paycheck every pay period. The government assumes how much money you will make during the entire year based on previous year's tax returns and current salary estimates, and then taxes you at the appropriate tax rate.

Every April when you file your tax returns, if everything was correct throughout the previous year, you should not owe the IRS anything and they should not owe you anything. There is a general misconception from some people that April is a time to get "free" money back from the government. If you receive money from the IRS, that means your tax estimates throughout the previous year were incorrect and you actually overpaid your taxes and now the IRS is correcting their mistake and reimbursing you. This is not necessarily a good thing; it means your money is being withheld from you for an entire year in which you could have been accumulating compound interest if you had it invested. On the other hand, if you owe the IRS a considerable amount of money, this means you were not paying your taxes correctly and the IRS could give you a fine for withholding their money for too long.

Let me get back to your paycheck. I am going to use round numbers in my explanations to make it easy to understand, but you can find more exact rates on official government websites. To get an understanding of federal income tax let's look at the tax rates per tax bracket. One common misunderstanding people have is that the more money you make, the more you get taxed, so sometimes it's better to make less money and get taxed less. On the contrary, the tax brackets are created equal for everyone, so yes you get taxed at a higher rate when you make more money, but your initial earnings before you get to the next tax bracket were taxed the same as everyone else.

Let me use some numbers to explain. We have Sara, who made $50,000 last year and Jessica, who made $90,000 last year. The lowest tax bracket in the US is from 0-$10,000 of earnings. Let's assume both Sara and Jessica are single (not married) and have no children (no dependents at all). So, for both of them, the first $10,000 of earnings they had last year were taxed at just a 10% rate. The government took $1,000 from each of them for the first $10,000 of earnings. They did the same for the likes of Bill Gates and Elon Musk too. Then we have the second bracket. The tax rate is 12% for earnings from $10,000 - $40,000. Even though Jessica made almost double the money that Sara did, she still got taxed at the same rate for the first $40,000 earned. In this bracket they each earned $30,000 and got taxed at 12%, so the government took $3,600 from each of them for federal income tax.

So far, they have each gotten taxed the same amount. The next tax bracket makes a big jump in rate. From $40,000-$85,000 of earnings, the federal government taxes you at 22%. Sara made $50,000 total last year, so she will be taxed at 22% just for the last $10,000 of earnings ($2,200 for her). Jessica will be taxed on her next $45,000 of earnings at that 22% rate. Meaning the government would take $9,900 out of her paychecks. The next bracket is from $85,000-$165,000 at a rate of 24%. Jessica's final $5,000 in earnings would be taxed at this 24% rate costing her $1,200 in taxes. I hope this clarifies how the federal income tax system is bracketed.

No matter how much money you earn per year as a whole, your beginning earnings are taxed the same as everyone else. You still make more money in total if you earn $86,000 and break into the 24% tax bracket vs. someone who only makes $84,000 and stays in the 22% tax bracket because only the last $1,000 in earnings was actually taxed at 24%. Long story short, the more money you earn, the more money you have to take home at the end of the day.

Back to looking at our paycheck, after that big chunk was deducted for federal income tax (and in some states, state income tax), now we see a section called "payroll taxes", first up is something that's called social security tax. Currently the social security tax rate is 12.4%. That tax gets split equal between employer and employee (you pay 6.2% and the company you work for pays 6.2%). If your paycheck was $4,000, you take on a 6.2% social security tax and would have $248 deducted from your check. Your employer has to match that amount and also pays $248 to the government.

Some of you are saying, what the heck? I do not even know what social security is and I don't want to pay for that. I won't go into the politics of social security, but the idea behind the system is that while you are young and working, you pay a little into the social security system every paycheck. A little here and a little there. Then when you are old and retired, the government sees that you paid into the system and will then write you checks every month repaying you what you paid since now you are no longer able to work. It is basically a government mandated retirement account. They take the money out of your paycheck for you and then when you get old, they give you the money back in the form of monthly checks for you to live out the rest of your life.

The social security tax does have a wage-based limit. The

limit is just around $140,000 of earnings. This means you get taxed at 6.2% until you start making over $140,000, then all your earnings past that are no longer subject to the tax. This kind of seems odd because wouldn't it make sense for the super-rich people to pay into the social security system even more since they have more money? Without giving my personal opinion on the matter, the idea of the wage-based limit was set because there is a maximum amount of money you can receive from the government when you retire in the form of social security checks. So, if there is a limit on what you can receive, then there is a limit on how much you can put in.

We (aka the US government) have been having problems with the social security system as of late in terms of it running out of funds soon, but I am just here to inform you what the tax is that you are paying and why. I'll let you do some other research and reading on how we intend to fix the system or maybe get rid of the system all together.

Back to the paycheck. You will also see a Medicare tax. This past year (2020) that tax was 2.9% split between employee and employer. If you made $4,000, you would have gotten a 1.45% tax deduction of $58 for the government to put towards the Medicare program. The Medicare program is put in place to help pay for hospital visits for the elderly and the disadvantaged. Again, the idea being that you pay into the system while you work and then when you retire, you can apply for Medicare and now get the benefits while the new generation works and pays into the system. There are a bunch of rules on retirement and amount of social security or Medicare benefits you receive based on how much you paid in and current age, but that can get very technical and is better left up to the government websites to explain.

What we want to know is how the tax system is working and where our money is going. The federal income tax will be used by the federal government across the board for things like education, social service programs, and defense/security of the nation. Taxes are a necessary evil. The government needs funding to keep us safe and build roads and parks and schools, etc., etc., but it does kind of stink when you think you are getting paid $4,000 a month and next thing you know; you only get to take home $3,200. Understanding the tax system is very useful when studying personal finance because you need to know how much money you actually will have in hand to spend and afterwards have to save and invest.

If you happen to be a 1099 employee instead of a W-2 employee, you will be required to pay taxes on your own instead of having them taken out of your paycheck. If you happen to be a 1099 independent contractor, you are supposed to pay taxes (aka write a check to the IRS) every quarter (aka every 3 months) based on estimated yearly earnings. It may take a little extra effort, but in the end, it is the same system. Your side hustle would likely be 1099 earnings or maybe even cash earnings.

It could be beneficial to open an LLC or some type of business depending on how much money you are bringing in and what kind of write-offs you may want to include based on your type of business. These subjects start to get a little farther away from basic personal finance, but do not let the technical terms and process of opening a business corporation stop you from having a side hustle. It may seem like a lot of work, but plenty of people do it every year, proving that it is possible, and you can do it too. Do some research on tax breaks, write-offs, cash payment businesses, LLC options, and whatever else you may need to know when filing taxes. The system can be a little complex, but the more knowledge you have of the system, the better decisions you can make about filing your taxes correctly and in the most beneficial way.

CHAPTER 7

Insurance

Insurance is a subject that I would guess most people find boring. We pay for insurance on things like our home, car, and personal health. We pay, we pay, we pay, and then when something goes wrong, it takes forever to file a claim and get a resolution. The better that we understand the terminology used in the insurance realm, the better choices we can make when choosing a plan.

Health insurance has been a hot topic in the past few years and the laws seem to be constantly changing. That can confuse people and makes it difficult to decide what plan to buy or when to switch. Spending extra money on better health insurance could be the right decision for you. If you are at high risk of injury because of your job or if you have a family history of disease or if you do not live a very healthy lifestyle you may need to spend more on your health insurance. Being healthy and staying healthy is a huge benefit to reaching financial freedom. If you keep your body and your mind healthy, you avoid missing work, you avoid paying for medical bills, and you tend to be more motivated and happier overall.

One main reason for everyone to have some kind of health insurance is to avoid that huge medical bill during a random accident, or what the industry likes to call a "catastrophic event". Even if you are 25 years old and eat healthy and exercise all the time, there is still the chance that you could slip and fall or get caught up in a bad situation at the wrong time. The odds of some of these events are very low, but in the off chance they happen to you, the cost is super high. Your hospital bill could easily be $300,000-$400,000 in total after scans and tests and days in the hospital bed

WORK HARD. SAVE HARD. INVEST HARD.

and even something like physical therapy afterwards. So, it does make sense for most people, if not all people, to at least have the minimum coverage to avoid these crazy hospital bills. A slip and fall accident could cost you your life savings, so we should use health insurance to avoid that scenario.

Let's go over some terms to be aware of when choosing a health insurance option. Monthly Premium: this is your monthly payment to the insurance company whether you make a claim (e.g. go to the hospital) or not. You could call up an insurance company and they will ask you your age, where you live, your weight, do you smoke, are you pregnant, etc., etc. and then based on their algorithm, will spit out a bunch of different options. Maybe your monthly premium choices would be $200, $300, or $400 a month.

Next, you will see the "deductible". The deductible is the amount of money you will pay out of pocket before the insurance company starts to help you pay. So, you pay your monthly premium no matter what, then if you do go to the hospital, you also pay for any bills until you reach your deductible amount. The higher the monthly premium, the lower the deductible and vice versa.

So, let's say the $200 premium has a $5,000 deductible, the $300 premium has a $3,000 deductible and the $400 premium has a $1,000 deductible. If you are healthy and rarely see the doctor, you probably want to take the lowest monthly premium and risk having a high deductible because you think the odds are that you won't go see the doctor at all. In that scenario, you pay $200 a month, $2,400 a year, so you can sleep at night knowing that if something catastrophic randomly happens to you, you will not lose your entire life savings or worse, go into debt. On the other hand, if you have a pre-existing condition or live a risky/ unhealthy lifestyle, you might take the high premium with low deductible knowing that you will get to the deductible spend amount fairly quickly each year and the insurance company can help pay the rest after that. Your deductible amount resets back to zero each year.

Then we have "co-pay" or co-payment. A co-pay is the fixed

amount you and I pay for regular, common visits to the doctor. Maybe our co-pays are $30 for a doctor visit, $75 for a hospital visit, and $20 for prescription drug pick-up. You will find more specific rules on co-pays per healthcare provider. Some may allow your co-pay to go towards your deductible and some may not. The co-pay amounts will fluctuate on different plans based on their monthly premiums and deductibles. If you receive a prescription drug on a regular basis, you may want to pay extra attention to that particular co-pay.

Lastly, we have co-insurance. This is one we need to pay extra attention to. You may see a "good deal" with a low monthly premium and a low deductible, but you forget to check the co-insurance percentage. Co-insurance is the percentage amount of a hospital bill you pay even after paying the full deductible. You really can see anything from 0-90% co-insurance. And that is a huge swing on what you might expect to pay out of pocket.

Let's use an example; you slip and fall and break your arm. You go to the hospital and your final bill is $40,000. If you picked one of those high premium, low deductible plans with no or 0% co-insurance, you're in good shape. Your monthly premium might have been $400, but if your deductible was only $1,000 and you have 0% co-insurance then you leave the hospital just needing to pay $1,000 and the insurance company pays the rest. However, if you thought you were getting a deal with a $200 monthly premium, $5,000 deductible and 50% co-insurance plan (because you were saving $200/month on the premium), now when you get that same bill, you have to pay the $5,000 deductible and 50% of the rest of the bill ($35,000/2 = $17,500). After thinking you were saving a bit of money on the monthly payment, now you're on the hook for $22,500. If you had that same plan but the co-insurance was also 0%, then you would be only paying $5,000, so be aware of what choices you are making.

Car insurance is another subject that is necessary to be well versed in. Let's assume it is mandatory for all drivers in the US to have car insurance. The laws are actually by state and there are some exceptions, but I will let you do additional research to find out if those options even apply to you and if they make any sense for you to obtain. More often than not, anyone who plans on owning and operating a vehicle must have proof of insurance. Car insurance should protect you against outrageous repair and hospital bills in the case of an accident, but probably the more important part is that it saves you from being sued directly by someone who you may have injured while driving. It is beneficial to that person you may have injured as well because if you were broke and they sued you, they would not get any money and have to pay their own medical bills, but having the car insurance company in the middle gives them a chance to have their medical bills paid for as well.

You do not want to overpay for car insurance, but you also want to make sure you are covered in case of an accident, theft, vandalism, or fire. When looking at your car insurance policy options, first you will probably see liability coverage. This is broken down into two sections. You have property damage, the amount of coverage the insurance company will pay for if there is damage to the vehicle or property of the person you hit. A common amount for this liability coverage is $100,000. So, if you hit a $20,000 car and totaled it, you're covered. The real trouble would be if you caused a pileup on the highway of let's say 5 Lamborghinis. That $100,000 worth of coverage could be spent rather quickly.

Next up, bodily injury; this is the amount of coverage your insurance company will cover for medical expenses of the person or people you hit (including potential income loss of the person injured and pain and suffering payouts if severe and sued). The bodily injury section is usually split into an amount per person covered, let's say $100,000 and an amount per occurrence covered, $300,000. Again, you're in good shape unless you caused severe damage to multiple people within the same accident.

You will see a section that helps cover you in the case that you get hit by someone who is not insured at all or underinsured. If someone hits your car and causes injury to you, but then you find out they are driving without insurance, you want to have some coverage where your own insurance company can help pay for the property damage or medical bills.

After that, you have comprehensive insurance that will cover incidentals, not collisions. An incidental could be flood damage, vandalism, a branch of a tree falling onto your hood, and plenty of other odds and ends. Be sure to read the fine print on this section as different companies cover different incidentals. Also, this section will come with a deductible, much like your health insurance. If your car was flooded and the repairs were $2,500, if your deductible is $1,000 for comprehensive insurance, you pay $1,000 and the insurance company pays the remaining $1,500.

Similarly, you have collision insurance. This will cover damage to your own vehicle in an accident caused by you or caused by someone else. Again, this portion will come with a deductible as well. By this point you are well on your way to making a sound decision about car insurance. You may see some more options such as car rental reimbursement, towing, or personal injury protection (PIP). Some are self-explanatory and some are state by state differences based on fault or no-fault state laws. I urge you to do some research on your particular state laws and always ask questions to your insurance company when you do not understand what you are purchasing.

As with these first two examples of insurance, homeowner's insurance is another one that will help protect a potential catastrophic event from ruining your investment of your home. Homeowners insurance will cover damage to your house, your property, and your belongings on the property. In some cases, it will also cover any possible damage or injury you may be responsible for involving another person on your property. Be aware of your coverage, as you may need to supplement your coverage with separate flood, earthquake, hurricane, or other insurance policy if you are in an area where some of these events are more common. Almost every mortgage company will force you to have homeowner's insurance, so unless you're paying cash for your home, expect to do some research and choose a policy. It is important to realize that most policies will not cover things such as mold, rust, termites, or corrosion. Therefore, it is in your best interest to keep your home clean and maintained throughout your ownership.

You may encounter other types of insurance not mentioned here, but now you are equipped with the knowledge to understand your options and ask questions when you need clarification.

CHAPTER 8

Food for Thought

Financial freedom is attainable. Through repetition, you can teach your brain to be financially responsible. Think before you spend. Set goals for your savings and investments. Find a system that works for you. Work hard. Save hard. Invest hard.

Start by realizing you must live beneath your means in order to save. If you spend all the money you earn, you can never reach financial freedom. Limit your risks until you have more financial stability. Try to avoid scenarios where you will be tempted to spend unnecessary money. See the big picture, play the long game.

You do not need to have a college degree to understand the basics of personal finance. In this simple book, you have gained enough knowledge to become wealthy. If you are willing to work hard and make decisions about money that may not be the "popular choice" or the "cool thing", you can reach your goals.

If you are already in financial trouble, I urge you to search for ways in which you can consolidate your debt and lower your interest payments. Pay back your debts before starting the process of saving and investing. Minimize your spending and maximize your earnings to pay back what you owe.

If you have any loans, be sure to make the payments on time. As with credit cards (which are loans too), you can really hurt your credit score by missing loan payments. Be responsible and be organized with your money.

Try not to be influenced by society, the media, and advertisements. Make your own, logical, educated decisions. Do some research before making large purchases or choosing insurance plans. Avoid people that bring you down or tell you that you can't do something. Be yourself. Surround yourself with people that have what you want. Ask questions. Always be learning.

Financial freedom can be reached a myriad of different ways. People will have different careers, live in different places, and enjoy different things, but no matter what, you will have to save and you will have to invest in something. Find a balance between enjoying life and obtaining financial freedom. Challenge yourself and enjoy the challenge.

Don't be discouraged by your age or your profession or your salary. We all had to start somewhere at some time and you can too. Most of my earnings have come from working at a restaurant. I did not own it, I did not have any family connection to it, and I did not have any specific special skill or any specific kind of degree or certification. I walked in one day looking for a job and they offered me one making sandwiches. 8 years later, here I am writing this book, living financially free. There is nothing that I did that you can't do. I hustled. I understood how to put my head down and work hard, how to set goals and save hard, and lastly, how to take those savings and invest hard.